You Are What You Eat

By
Shaykh Mufti Saiful Islām

© Copyright by JKN Publications

First Published in February 2019

ISBN: 978-1-909114-40-1

British Library Cataloguing in Publication Data
A catalogue record for this book is available from the British Library.

Publisher's Note:

Every care and attention has been put into the production of this book. If however you find any errors, they are our own, for which we seek Allāh's 襲 forgiveness and reader's pardon.

Published by:

JKN Publications
118 Manningham Lane
Bradford
West Yorkshire
BD8 7JF
United Kingdom

t: +44 (0) 1274 308 456 | w: www.jkn.org.uk | e: info@jkn.org.uk

Book Title: You Are What You Eat

Author: Shaykh Mufti Saiful Islām

Printed by Mega Printing in Turkey

"In the Name of Allāh, the Most Beneficent,
the Most Merciful"

Content

Introduction

All praises be to Allāh ﷻ, the Lord of the Worlds and may peace and blessings be showered upon the Final Messenger, Muhammad ﷺ, upon his noble Companions and upon those who follow their noble lifestyles until the final hour.

For many years in the past up until the present day the issue of Halāl and Harām has become sensitive and yet controversial amongst Muslims. Consumption of Harām or at least doubtful products have now become endemic in our Muslim community. Some of the basic reasons for this is the lack of concern that many Muslims have as well as ignorance of its importance and status in Islām. Furthermore, many Muslims show carelessness in primarily investigating or at least consulting with the scholars on this matter. There are ample amount of verses in the Holy Qur'ān and Ahādīth that emphasise on this issue which is why the prominent Jurists of the past have elaborated on this subject in depth for the benefit of the Muslim Ummah. Just as Salāh, Fasting, Zakāt, Hajj etc are obligatory upon us, similarly consuming Halāl and earning a lawful income is mandatory upon us.

Eating Halāl and earning a lawful income plays a vital role in the acceptance of all our Ibādāt (worship) and good deeds. A person can never attain the status of piety if one is careless in this matter. In fact, it was amongst the noble practices of our pious predecessors that not only did they refrain from Harām products but were equally very cautious regarding doubtful products.

Mufti Saiful Islām Sāhib has presented a discourse on this matter in one of his talks. I found the discourse to be very beneficial, informative and enlightening on the subject of Halāl and Harām that clarifies its importance and status in Islām. I strongly recommend my Muslim brothers and sisters to read this treatise and to study it thoroughly. This discourse was kindly transcribed by Sister Munira Islām, one of the female students of JKN. May Allāh ﷻ bless this student in her studies, and make it a means of salvation for her in the hereafter. I pray to Allāh ﷻ to benefit us all from this treatise and to facilitate our understanding on this matter.

Āmīn Yā Rabbal-Ālamīn.

Mufti Abdul Waheed
Teacher at JKN, December 2009

Islām – A Complete Religion

Respected listeners, Alhamdulillāh, Allāh ﷻ has given us this opportunity to congregate and learn about His Dīn; learn about His commandments and prohibitions. We must realise that Islām is a complete religion and a complete way of life. It governs us, teaches us and directs us to achieve success in this world and in the hereafter. Islām has the solution to all our modern day problems, difficulties, hardships and Masā'il (juristic issues). There exists no aspect of life that is not included in its teachings and moral guidelines.

Unfortunately, many of us today do not consider Islām in the matters of marriage, social affairs, economics and politics. We conduct business as we please, buying and selling any commodity as we wish. Many of us seek employment at any institution without paying the slightest heed to whether the employment is Halāl or Harām. Allāh ﷻ states in Sūrah Al-Baqarah,

يَآأَيُّهَاالَّذِيْنَ اٰمَنُوا ادْخُلُوْا فِى السِّلْمِ كَآفَّةً وَّلَا تَتَّبِعُوْا خُطُوَاتِ الشَّيْطَانِ اِنَّهٗ لَكُمْ عَدُوٌّ مُّبِيْنٌ

"O you who believe, enter into Islām completely and do not follow the footsteps of Shaytān, for verily he is your clear enemy."(2:208)

This particular verse was revealed regarding certain Companions ﷺ who had reverted from Judaism to Islām but wished to uphold some of their Judaic traditions such as to honour Saturday and abstain from consuming camel's meat. They also informed the Holy Prophet ﷺ that since the Tawrah was the book of Allāh ﷻ, they re-

7

cited it in their Tahajjud Salāh. Allāh ﷻ revealed the above verse on this occasion, instructing them that after the advent of Islām no other religion should be adhered to.

(Ad-Durrul Manthūr and Baydāwi)

Islām – A Religion for All

The aforementioned verse also instructs every Muslim to embrace all the commandments of Islām and practice them accordingly irrespective of their status. This is binding upon the ruler and the subject, the big and the small, the employer and employee, the businessman and the farmer alike. Allāh ﷻ our Creator, our Lord, our Master loves us immensely and is very Compassionate towards us. He states in the Holy Qur'ān,

$$هُوَ الَّذِىْ خَلَقَ لَكُمْ مَّا فِى الْاَرْضِ جَمِيْعًا$$

"It is He Who created for you all that is on the earth." (2:29)

There is no doubt that everything on the earth is created for our advantage but He also states in other verses;

$$يَاۤ اَيُّهَا الَّذِيْنَ اٰمَنُوْا كُلُوْا مِمَّا فِى الْاَرْضِ حَلَالًا طَيِّبًا وَ لَا تَتَّبِعُوْا خُطُوَاتِ الشَّيْطَانِ اِنَّهٗ لَكُمْ عَدُوٌّ مُّبِيْنٌ$$

"O Mankind; eat from that which is lawful (Halāl) and good on earth and follow not the footsteps of Shaytān. Verily, he is your clear enemy." (2:168)

$$يَاۤ اَيُّهَا الَّذِيْنَ اٰمَنُوْا لَا تُحَرِّمُوْا طَيِّبٰتِ مَاۤ اَحَلَّ اللهُ لَكُمْ وَ لَا تَعْتَدُوْا اِنَّ اللهَ لَا يُحِبُّ$$

الْمُعْتَدِيْنَ وَكُلُوْا مِمَّا رَزَقَكُمُ اللهُ حَلَالًا طَيِّبًا وَاتَّقُوا اللهَ الَّذِىٓ اَنْتُمْ بِه مُؤْمِنُوْنَ

"O you who believe, make not Harām (unlawful) the pure (all that is good regards to food, deeds, beliefs, persons etc) which Allāh has made lawful (Halāl) for you and transgress not, verily Allāh does not like the transgressors. Eat from the lawful (Halāl) and pure sustenance which Allāh has provided for you, and fear Allāh in Whom you believe." (5:87-88)

Therefore we need to be careful about what we consume, identifying whether it is Halāl or Harām.

Abstaining from Harām

When Allāh ﷻ announced the completion of His Dīn on the occasion of Hajjatul-Wida (farewell Hajj), in addition, He also mentioned some unlawful things for protecting our bodily system. Allāh ﷻ states in the Holy Qur'ān,

حُرِّمَتْ عَلَيْكُمُ الْمَيْتَةُ وَالدَّمُ وَلَحْمُ الْخِنْزِيْرِ وَمَا أُهِلَّ لِغَيْرِ اللهِ بِه وَالْمُنْخَنِقَةُ وَالْمَوْقُوْذَةُ وَالْمُتَرَدِّيَةُ وَالنَّطِيْحَةُ وَمَا أَكَلَ السَّبُعُ إِلَّا مَا ذَكَّيْتُمْ وَمَا ذُبِحَ عَلَى النُّصُبِ وَأَنْ تَسْتَقْسِمُوْا بِالْأَزْلَامِ ذٰلِكُمْ فِسْقٌ اَلْيَوْمَ يَئِسَ الَّذِيْنَ كَفَرُوْا مِنْ دِيْنِكُمْ فَلَا تَخْشَوْهُمْ وَاخْشَوْنِ اَلْيَوْمَ اَكْمَلْتُ لَكُمْ دِيْنَكُمْ وَاَتْمَمْتُ عَلَيْكُمْ نِعْمَتِىْ وَرَضِيْتُ لَكُمُ الْإِسْلَامَ دِيْنًا.

"The things which are forbidden for you are; Maytah (dead animal), blood, flesh of swine (pork) and that on which Allāh's name has not been mentioned while slaughtering (or what has been slaughtered with the name of another besides Allāh). And

9

(also prohibited are those animals that are) strangled to death, violently beaten, fallen (from high place), or gored to death and what has been partly eaten by a predator unless you are able to slaughter it (before its death). And that (animal) which has been slaughtered at the altars (stone shrines) and (also forbidden) is to use arrows seeking decision. (All) these are acts of sin. This day those who have disbelieved have relinquished all hope of your religion (Islām) so fear them not, but fear Me. This day I have perfected your religion for you, and completed My favour upon you and have chosen for you Islām as your religion." (5:3)

Allāh ﷻ also states,

$$ اَلْيَوْمَ أُحِلَّ لَكُمُ الطَّيِّبْتُ $$

"This day, all kinds of pure things have become lawful for you." (5:5)

The aforementioned verses express the importance of consuming Halāl and abstaining from Harām to the extent that Allāh ﷻ reiterates the declaration of certain categories of meat to be prohibited along with the mentioning of perfection of our beautiful religion, Islām.

Command Upon the Prophets ﷺ to Consume Halāl

Similarly Allāh ﷻ states in another verse,

$$ يَا أَيُّهَا الرُّسُلُ كُلُوا مِنَ الطَّيِّبْتِ وَاعْمَلُوا صَالِحًا إِنِّي بِمَا تَعْمَلُونَ عَلِيمٌ $$

10

"O Messengers, eat of the Tayyibāt (all kinds of Halāl foods), and do righteous deeds. Verily, I am aware of what you do." (23:51)

The most beloved people to Allāh ﷻ are His noble Messengers. If Allāh ﷻ has instructed them to eat pure and Halāl food and to do righteous deeds, then how important will it be for the believers? In this verse, there is a unique connection between the consumption of Halāl food and the performance of righteous deeds. Allāh ﷻ first commences with the command of consuming Halāl food and thereafter the performing of righteous deeds.

The more pure the food is, the better the good deed will be. Allāh ﷻ will enable a person to carry out good deeds due to consuming Halāl and pure food. Halāl food plays a great influence in our worship too. If food, clothes and other belongings are not lawful then our worship will be affected as well.

Why our Du'ās are not Accepted

عَنْ أَبِي هُرَيْرَةَ، قَالَ: قَالَ رَسُولُ اللهِ صَلَّى اللهُ عَلَيْهِ وَسَلَّمَ: أَيُّهَا النَّاسُ، إِنَّ اللهَ طَيِّبٌ لَا يَقْبَلُ إِلَّا طَيِّبًا، وَإِنَّ اللهَ أَمَرَ الْمُؤْمِنِينَ بِمَا أَمَرَ بِهِ الْمُرْسَلِينَ، فَقَالَ: يَا أَيُّهَا الرُّسُلُ كُلُوا مِنَ الطَّيِّبَاتِ وَاعْمَلُوا صَالِحًا. إِنِّي بِمَا تَعْمَلُونَ عَلِيمٌ وَقَالَ: يَا أَيُّهَا الَّذِينَ آمَنُوا كُلُوا مِنْ طَيِّبَاتِ مَا رَزَقْنَاكُمْ ثُمَّ ذَكَرَ الرَّجُلَ يُطِيلُ السَّفَرَ أَشْعَثَ أَغْبَرَ، يَمُدُّ يَدَيْهِ إِلَى السَّمَاءِ، يَا رَبِّ، يَا رَبِّ، وَمَطْعَمُهُ حَرَامٌ، وَمَشْرَبُهُ حَرَامٌ، وَمَلْبَسُهُ حَرَامٌ، وَغُذِيَ بِالْحَرَامِ، فَأَنَّى يُسْتَجَابُ لَهُ (رواه مسلم)

Sayyidunā Abū Hurairah ﷺ narrated that the Messenger of Allāh ﷺ said, "Allāh ﷻ is pure and accepts only which is pure and Allāh ﷻ has commanded the faithful to do that which He has commanded the Messengers. Allāh ﷻ states, **"O Messengers! Eat from the pure things and do righteous deeds."** He also states, **"O you who believe! Eat from the pure things which We have provided you."** Then he (the Holy Prophet ﷺ) mentioned a man, having travelled for a long distance, dishevelled hair and covered in dust who raises his hands towards the sky exclaiming; "O My Lord, O My Lord!" whilst his food is Harām, his drink is Harām and his clothing is Harām, so how could he expect his Du'ā to be answered?" (Muslim)

This Hadīth clearly illustrates the importance of eating Halāl, earning Halāl livelihood and refraining from all types of Harām and doubtful sources. Consuming and earning Halāl is one of the vital factors for our supplications to be accepted by Allāh ﷻ.

Halāl and Harām are Clear

Our religion Islām has made matters very clear. It is narrated by Sayyidunā Nu'mān Ibn Bashīr ﷺ that the Holy Prophet ﷺ said,

اَلْحَلَالُ بَيِّنٌ، وَالْحَرَامُ بَيِّنٌ وَبَيْنَهُمَا أُمُوْرٌ مُشْتَبِهَةٌ، فَمَنْ تَرَكَ مَا شُبِّهَ عَلَيْهِ مِنَ الْإِثْمِ، كَانَ لِمَا اسْتَبَانَ أَتْرَكَ، وَمَنِ اجْتَرَأَ عَلَى مَا يَشُكُّ فِيْهِ مِنَ الْإِثْمِ، أَوْشَكَ أَنْ يُوَاقِعَ مَا اسْتَبَانَ، وَالْمَعَاصِيْ حِمَى اللهِ مَنْ يَرْتَعْ حَوْلَ الْحِمٰى يُوْشِكُ أَنْ يُوَاقِعَهُ (رواه البخارى)

"Halāl is clear and Harām is clear, and between them are unclear (doubtful) matters. So whosoever forsakes those doubtful matters lest he may commit a sin, will definitely avoid what is clearly un-lawful, and whosoever indulges in these doubtful things openly is likely to commit that which is clearly unlawful. Sins are Allāh's ﷻ Himā (i.e. private pasture) and whoever grazes (his sheep) near it, is likely to trespass over it. (Bukhāri)

Abstaining from Doubtful Matters

Imām Tirmizi ﷻ has recorded a Hadīth regarding doubtful matters that is worth implementing into our everyday lives pertaining to income, food, clothing and all other matters. He narrates on the au-thority of Sayyidunā Hasan Ibn Ali ؓ that the Holy Prophet ﷺ said,

دَعْ مَا يُرِيْبُكَ اِلٰى مَا لَا يُرِيْبُكَ

"Leave that which puts you in doubt and do that in which you have no doubt." (Tirmizi)

If we apply this golden principle into our daily lives then how easy will everything become? Alhamdulillāh, there are many types of food available which are Halāl and not doubtful. It only requires us to restrain our Nafs and desires from transgressing towards doubtful and Harām foods.

If we for a moment observe the lives of the Holy Prophet ﷺ and his noble Sahābah ؓ, we will acknowledge how they abstained from Harām and how precautious they were in doubtful substances. They are exemplary role models for our Muslims today especially concerning doubtful issues. Their habits and traits as a whole are

13

worth following, as they were the people specially chosen by Allāh ﷻ to be the Companions of His beloved Prophet ﷺ. The Holy Prophet ﷺ said, "I have been sent in the best period of human history." The time of the Holy Prophet ﷺ was itself a blessed period, and those that were honoured with his companionship were in fact the cream of that age.

The Holy Prophet's ﷺ Sleepless Night

It is mentioned in the books of Ahādīth that once the Holy Prophet ﷺ had a sleepless night. He would turn from side to side and could not sleep. His noble wife asked him, "O Prophet of Allāh ﷺ! Why can't you sleep?" He replied, "A date was lying about, I took it and ate it, lest it should be wasted, now I am troubled lest it might be from Sadaqah."

Sadaqah whether monetary or food was not permissible for the Holy Prophet ﷺ and his noble family. Most probably, the date belonged to the Prophet ﷺ himself, but because people sent him their Sadaqah (for distribution), he consequently could not sleep with the apprehension that it might be from Sadaqah. It was due to the fear of Allāh ﷻ that he was sleepless during the night. It is ironic for those who assert to be the followers of the Holy Prophet ﷺ yet indulge in Harām affairs such as unlawful business, usury, corruption, theft etc.

The Holy Prophet ﷺ Accepts a Woman's Invitation

On another occasion, the Holy Prophet ﷺ was returning from a fu-

14

neral when a woman approached him and requested him to partake in some food in her house. He went in with some of his noble Sahābah ﷺ. When the food was served, the Holy Prophet ﷺ took a morsel and began to chew it but it would simply not go down his throat. He remarked, "It seems that the animal has been slaughtered without the permission of its owner." The woman replied, "O Messenger of Allāh ﷺ, I had requested a man to purchase a goat for me from the market, but he could not obtain one. My neighbour had purchased a goat. Therefore, I sent the man there with some money to buy it from them. My neighbour's husband was out so his wife handed over the goat to him."

The Holy Prophet ﷺ directed her to go and serve the meal to the captives. It is reported from certain biographers regarding the pious servants of Allāh ﷺ that food obtained from doubtful sources would simply not go down their throats. Therefore, this is not a surprising fact regarding the Holy Prophet ﷺ who attained the highest degree of piety.

Sayyidunā Abū Bakr ﷺ and a Soothsayer's Food

It is reported that Sayyidunā Abū Bakr ﷺ once had a slave who used to give him a portion of his daily income as the master's share. Once he brought him some food and Sayyidunā Abū Bakr ﷺ took a morsel out of it. The slave remarked, "You always primarily enquire of the source of what I bring to you, but today you have not done so." He replied, "I was feeling so hungry that I failed to do that. Tell me now where did you purchase this food?" The slave replied, "Before I had embraced Islām, I practised soothsaying.

15

During those days, I came across some people for whom I practiced some of my charms. They promised to pay me later on. I happened to pass by those same people today and while they were engaged in a marriage ceremony, they gave me this food." Sayyidunā Abū Bakr ◈ exclaimed, "Ah you would have surely destroyed me!"

Then he tried to vomit the morsel he had swallowed, but he could not do so as his stomach had been quiet empty. Someone suggested that he drinks water to his fill then try to vomit. He sent for a big glass of water and kept on drinking and vomiting until the morsel came out. Somebody remarked, "May Allāh ﷻ have mercy upon you, you put yourself through so much trouble for one morsel." To this he replied, "I would have thrust it out even if I had to lose my life, for I have heard the Holy Prophet ﷺ saying, "The flesh nourished by Harām food is destined for the Fire of Hell." I therefore made haste to vomit this morsel, lest any portion of my body would become nourished by it."

Many stories of this nature have been reported about Sayyidunā Abū Bakr ◈. Out of caution, he never consumed anything unless he was certain of its source. Even the slightest doubt of it being Halāl would cause him to vomit what he had taken in.

Sayyidunā Umar ◈ Vomits out the Milk of Sadaqah

An incident occurred with Sayyidunā Umar ◈ that a person brought him some milk. When he took it, he noted its unusual taste and asked the person how it had come into his possession. He replied, "The camels given in Sadaqah were grazing in the desert and the attendants gave me this milk out of what they got from them." When Sayyidunā Umar ❀ heard this, he took his hand inside his mouth and vomited what he had taken in. Such God-fearing people not only abstained from Harām food, but were also most anxious to avoid any doubtful morsel finding its way inside them. They could not possibly consume anything that was Harām, which is so normal these days.

Imām Abū Hanīfah's ❀ Piety

Abdullāh Ibn Mubārak ❀ relates, "On one occasion a few stolen goats were found amongst the goats of Kūfa. On hearing this, Imām Abū Hanīfah ❀ enquired about the maximum age of a goat. When informed that goats normally live for up to seven years, he abstained from eating goat meat for seven years."

In one of his biographies, it is mentioned about Imām Sāhib ❀ witnessing a solider who after consuming a piece of meat disposed the remainder in a river in Kūfa. Imām Sāhib ❀ made enquiries about how long a fish lives. The people informed him of a certain period, and thus he abstained from eating fish for that entire period.

Just ponder over the incidents of our pious predecessors. How much sacrifice they underwent to safeguard themselves from consuming Harām or even doubtful nourishment. After all, you are what you eat. Hence, such people became the guiding and illuminating stars in this world and will be in the hereafter.

17

An Incident of Imām Shāfi'ī 🕮 and Imām Ahmad Ibn Hanbal 🕮

Once Imām Ahmad Ibn Hanbal 🕮 became the guest of Imām Shāfi'ī 🕮. Although Imām Ahmad 🕮 was a student of Imām Shāfi'ī 🕮, the latter used to honour and respect the former immensely. Thus, Imām Shāfi'ī 🕮 ordered his daughter to prepare the finest food and show great hospitality towards the great Imām. She complied with her father's wishes, yet in the morning when the great Imām departed from their house, the daughter complained to her father.

She stated, "You mentioned that he was a great Imām and saint, however I found three things contrary to his piety. Firstly, he ate a lot of food whereas pious people eat less food. Secondly, he did not perform Tahajjud Salāh and thirdly, and the most serious of all, is that he performed Fajr Salāh without Wudhu." Imām Shāfi'ī 🕮 initially reprimanded her for making such remarks but he himself in private related the incident to Imām Ahmad Ibn Hanbal 🕮.

Imām Ahmad 🕮 replied, "Firstly, the reason I ate plentiful was that the food was purely one-hundred percent Halāl, as I observed the Barakah, Nūr and blessings on the Dastarkhān (table cloth) which I did not observe anywhere else. Hence the more I ate, the more Barakah and blessings I acquired.

Secondly, I stayed awake throughout the night deriving and deducing Masā'il from the Holy Qur'ān and Ahādīth. I managed to derive seventeen Masā'il for the Muslim Ummah. Despite Tahajjud being an act of Ibādah, its benefits are restricted only to myself

18

whereas the deriving of Masā'il is not only beneficial and rewardable for me but for the Muslim Ummah also. So the rewards are greater for this action, thus I did not perform Tahajjud Salāh.

Thirdly, I did not perform Fajr Salāh without Wudhu because I remained awake throughout the entire night deriving Masā'il (and nothing that breaches Wudhu took place), hence the Wudhu remained intact, so therefore I performed Fajr Salāh with the Wudhu of Ishā Salāh." Subhān-Allāh!

Consuming Halāl enables a person to perform virtuous and righteous deeds as well. The more pure the food is, the better and greater the Ibādah will be and therefore the closer one will be to Allāh 🕮.

Halāl Stickers

Therefore, my dear brothers and sisters, if this was the state of such pious servants of Allāh 🕮 then what level have we plunged to? We have not bothered to put any emphasis on this very important matter. How confident are we that what we are eating is Halāl if we do not express any concern about it? Especially with recent reports that have been published exposing some products to be labelled as Halāl whilst containing traces of pork? Considering this, will the Halāl sticker on the product or on the shop window be sufficient to justify it being Halāl?

Prophecy of the Holy Prophet 🕮

The Holy Prophet 🕮 had prophesised regarding this inevitable dilemma more than 1400 years ago. The Hadīth is found in Sahīh Bukhāri narrated by Sayyidunā Abū Hurairah ؓ that the Holy Prophet ﷺ said,

يَأْتِى عَلَى النَّاسِ زَمَانٌ لَا يُبَالِى الْمَرْءُ مَا أَخَذَ مِنْهُ أَمِنَ الْحَلَالِ أَمْ مِّنَ الْحَرَامِ

"A time will come upon the people when one will not care how one gains (ones money, food, clothing etc) either through a Halāl or Harām source."

In another Hadīth narrated by Imām Ahmad ؓ in his Musnad on the authority of Sayyidunā Sa'd Ibn Abi Waqqās ؓ that the Holy Prophet ﷺ said,

لَا تَقُوْمُ السَّاعَةُ حَتَّى يَخْرُجَ قَوْمٌ يَأْكُلُوْنَ بِأَلْسِنَتِهِمْ كَمَا تَأْكُلُ الْبَقَرَةُ بِأَلْسِنَتِهَا

"The Day of Judgement will not come until there will be such people who will eat with their tongues just as cows eat with their tongues."

Unfortunately, we are witnessing this within our Muslim community, consuming anything and everything without the slightest fear of its source. Remember my brothers and sisters, it is our duty and obligation to carry out a thorough investigation to the best of our ability of the food that we consume. The Hadīth of Baihaqi clearly states,

لَا يَدْخُلُ الْجَنَّةَ جَسَدٌ غُذِىَ بِالْحَرَامِ

"That individual will not enter Paradise that has been nourished with Harām."

We have to make this matter very clear even with regards to Halāl livelihood as it is mentioned in the Hadīth of Mishkāt,

طَلَبُ كَسْبِ الْحَلَالِ فَرِيْضَةٌ بَعْدَ الْفَرِيْضَةِ

"Earning a Halāl livelihood is an obligation after the other obligations."

As Salāh, Fasting, Hajj and Zakāt are obligatory upon us, similarly, earning Halāl income is also obligatory upon us. Remember, we will be questioned on the Day of Judgement about the food that we consumed, whether it was Halāl or Harām, and whether we fed our families Halāl or not. Imām Bukhāri ﷺ and Imām Muslim ﷺ have narrated a Hadīth;

اَلَا كُلُّكُمْ رَاعٍ وَكُلُّكُمْ مَّسْئُوْلٌ عَنْ رَعِيَّتِه

"Be aware! Every one of you is a shepherd and every one of you will be questioned about his herd."

Therefore, each one of us is a custodian and each one of us will be questioned about our subordinates. Let us prepare ourselves before it is too late. Let us awaken ourselves from the slumber of laziness, neglect and complacency and acknowledge the reality.

May Allāh ﷻ give us all the ability to consume Halāl food, earn a Halāl livelihood and may He through His infinite grace save us from all types of Harām food, Harām livelihood and doubtful things. Āmīn!

Over Eating

A common pastime in today's modern Muslim society is eating as a social activity. Whether it be eating out at a restaurant, being invited to someone's house as a guest, or an invitation to a larger party. The act of meeting fellow Muslims and accepting invitations is encouraged in Islām.

As stated in the Hadīth, "The believer is the one who is sociable (with others) and there is no good in one who is not sociable (with others) nor in one who is not met sociably (by them)." (Baihaqi)

The reason for this is that it creates love and harmony between Muslims, allows healthy friendships to develop, and in turn creates a strong Muslim community. When we attend these events we feel good that we are partaking in Halāl, and the hope that Allāh ﷻ will reward us abundantly for participating.

Often, along with these pre-arranged meetings are the promises of a great feast, different varieties of fried food starters, a main course that consists of no less than three different options followed by generous helpings of a choice of desserts. There is high anticipation and excitement as the time draws near. Once present, we eat, enjoy and savour the vast array of delicious food being offered. We overfill our plates and go back for seconds and even thirds. We see others doing the same so our sense of shame or guilt at the explicit greediness we display is at the back of our minds.

Even knowing that the portions are simply too large to take down, we stuff ourselves beyond comfort. "All you can eat buffets" are a prime example, where so many have so easily fallen victim to overindulgence. In the current consumer climate, "all you can eat buffets" are value for money as long as you can stuff most of it down.

Allāh ﷻ warns us against over eating and advises us to be moderate in consumption. **"Eat and drink but do not waste, Allāh ﷻ does not love those who waste." (7:31)**

I know most of you will be thinking, "Oh I don't really eat to my fill" or "Its only once in a while" and that may be so. However, the rise in modern day illnesses and complaints such as diabetes, high blood pressure and heart disease are all directly linked to the immoderate and over consumption of food. Some of us have fallen into such a trap that if we don't eat to our fill, we don't feel satisfied.

The Holy Prophet ﷺ has clearly said, "Over eating does not go with good health." (Haythami)

Being aware of the effect our actions are having on the health of our body is the first step towards rectifying our eating habits.

Firstly, if we look towards the example and appearance of our beloved Prophet ﷺ, we can see his dislike for overeating on seeing an overweight man, he said, "If you did not have a large belly it would be better for you." [Haythami]

Imām Ghazāli ﷺ states in his Book of Destructive Evils, "Of all the evils which have descended from heaven to earth, the worst is eating to the hearts content."

The Holy Prophet ﷺ himself practiced moderation in eating which is evident from various narrations of the respected Sahābah ﷺ in the Shamāil of Imām Tirmizi ﷺ on the Holy Prophet's ﷺ appearance, he is reported to have had a flat stomach.

Along with the detriment over eating causes to ones health, some of us may already be seeing the effects it is having on other areas of our character and lifestyle.

Imām Ghazāli ﷺ has talked comprehensively about this in his Book of Destructive Evils. He lists the harms of over eating as:

- Laziness
- Excessive sleep
- Hard heartedness
- Power of memory becomes dull
- Thinking power falls asleep
- Wisdom becomes idle
- Bodily organs abstain from divine service
- Loss of attribute of showing kindness to people
- Pride
- Clash of interests
- Hatred

Only once we are conscious of our eating habits can we aim to rectify them. In the following two Ahādīth the Holy Prophet 🕮 has given practical advice to help guide us towards moderate eating habits.

"No human ever filled a vessel worse than the stomach. Sufficient for any son of Ādam are some morsels to keep his back straight. But if it must be, then one third for his food, one third for his drink and one third for his breath." (Ahmad, Tirmizi, Nasai, Ibn Mājah)

"Food for one is enough for two and food for two is enough for three and food for three is enough for four."
                                    (Ahmad, Tirmizi, Nasai, Ibn Mājah)
In summary, try to remember:

- Eat only when hungry
- Stop eating when hunger has gone (not when fullness is felt)
- Do not eat when bored
- Do not eat on the move
- Using smaller plates may help
- Eat consciously and chew slowly
- Sit on the floor in the Sunnah sitting position (not leaning or legs crossed)

Those of us with young children know that adopting these sensible and Sunnah eating habits are all the more important, so that we are an example for the good health of the next generation.

25

The great Imām Ghazāli ﷺ has advised parents in a simple and truly inspirational piece. He writes, "The first characteristic to take hold of a child is greed for food. It is essential to discipline him in this matter. He should be taught to despise over eating. This may be achieved by telling him that those who over eat are like animals, and censuring children who over eat in front of him, and praising those who exhibit good etiquette and eat conservatively. He should be taught to love sharing food, to attach little importance to it, and to be content with simple food, no matter what it is."

May Allāh ﷻ guide us all towards moderation, Āmīn!

Provide your Children with a Well-Balanced Diet

Every mother is required to pay special care towards their children's diet. Any deficiency in their nourishment adversely affects their physical and mental well being. We see a number of kids who, in-spite of hailing from affluent homes, appear lethargic and weak. On closer investigation we discovered that their mothers fed them with very delicious but non-nourishing food at the wrong time.

The child's stomach will get full with such food but he is being deprived of a diet that would maintain his physical and mental well being. If you want the child to be alert and healthy, pay special attention to his diet. Do not just feed him willy-nilly. Prepare a feeding chart or schedule. Children who are overfed or fed haphazardly tend to be relatively overweight. These obese children are then unable to jump, play and be energetic like other children of their age group. In fact, they tend to become mentally weak as well.

Some mothers grumble that their financial condition does not allow them to buy nourishing foodstuffs like almonds, pistachios etc. In response, we contend that you do not have to buy almonds, pistachios and the like. There are a number of other types of nourishing foods. Dieticians have analysed that even peanuts and chickpeas are the equivalent of or maybe better than almonds.

Prepare a well balanced diet chart for your child. It is fairly simple to prepare one. If you stick to the planned schedule of a well balanced diet, Inshā-Allāh, this will contribute tremendously to his alertness and his mental and his physical well being. He will play a meaningful role in society at large. If the food is wholly nutritional, the health of the physical body as well as the mind is maintained. Once the mind is healthy, its thoughts would also be healthy, the community will inevitably prosper. Corruption would be eliminated and a decent society will possibly come to pass.

So how pleasing it would be if each and every child received the official recommended amount of nutritional food daily. Within the homes, this responsibility rests on the parents shoulders and upon the shoulders of the government, in other establishments. The dilemma of malnourished children existing in the world is a plight that needs to be resolved with all resources and measures at our disposal.

Provide Your Children a Good Breakfast

Generally, many mothers do not give their children a very healthy breakfast. They regard tea and biscuits as an adequate meal. This does no good for the child's health. Such an inadequate meal will make him weak and affect his development. His body will lack the vital vitamins and calcium.

Therefore, an understanding mother with this intention that the child would grow up to be strong and healthy and through this he would spread the message of Dīn to every point on the globe should feed her children a nutritional breakfast. For example, she may feed them with milk, eggs, fruit etc.

A famous Persian expression reveals, "A morsel in the morning is better than chicken and fish."

In other words, a little bit of food early in the morning is far better than thousands of other blessings. In ancient forms of medicine, a good breakfast was very strongly recommended because the whole day hinged on breakfast. If a person has a good nutritional breakfast, there would not be a problem even if he has a very light snack for lunch. Therefore, we should feed our children and ourselves as well, according to our ability, with a good, wholesome and nutritional breakfast. Very starchy or oily foods are detrimental to the health. Fried food is harmful particularly to children who have to sit at school all day long. With the children's intense physical training, even these foods may digest rapidly (leaving them hungry again). So avoid these foods for breakfast, prepare a daily breakfast menu that is both appetising as well as nutritious. Whilst preparing your menu, take into account the seasons as well. A half boiled egg for example is very appetising and beneficial to the health.

Add the juice of a freshly squeezed lemon to water (1/2 a lemon to a glass of water). Feed this juice to your children and you too should drink it.

This is very beneficial to the throat and the eyes. Similarly, carrots are good for the eyesight and it also increases the blood.

Apart from this, the primary ingredient of a good breakfast is cereal. Most homes do not even bother about it. Cereals are filled with vitamins and minerals. Cereals are a good source of nutrition and their nutritional value is further increased when milk is added. Make the cereals a must in your breakfast. The cereals need to be changed from time to time otherwise the child will get fed up eating the same cereal daily.

Medicine Containing Harām Ingredients

Q I have recently discovered that the insulin used by diabetics to maintain their sugar level is obtained from the pancreas of a pig. Would this be acceptable (i.e. to use this insulin) under Islamic law, considering the fact that the diabetic needs the insulin to maintain his sugar level for survival and pain relief? To the best of my knowledge, there is no alternative. Please can you provide me with any evidence from the Holy Qur'ān and Ahādīth?

A It is stated in the Holy Qur'ān, "He (Allāh) has forbidden for you, only the Maytah (dead animal), blood, the flesh of swine and that which is slaughtered as a sacrifice for other than Allāh (has been slaughtered for idols etc.). However, if one is forced by necessity, neither rebelliously nor transgressing the limits, then there is no sin for him. Truly Allāh is Forgiving and Most Merciful." (2:173)

From this verse an injunction can be deduced that to use forbidden products for medical purposes in exceptional circumstances, is permissible. Under the following extreme conditions prohibited medicine become permissible:

1.   In a critical state where life is in danger.
2.   The health is so critical that by not consuming such medicine, the health will severely deteriorate permanently.
3.   There is no alternative Halāl medicine available.
4.   The Harām medicine used is effective as a cure for that partic-

ular illness or disease.

5. There is no carnal desire involved during the usage of the Harām product other than for the cure.

6. Only the amount needed should be used without exceeding the limits.

7. An expert doctor informs that there is no alternative cure other than that medicine.

If all the aforementioned conditions are met, then in such a critical condition, Harām products can be used for medical purpose. However, in this day and age, because the usage of Harām medicine are endemically found, the Fuqahā (jurists) have given permission to use them in usual conditions of illness when no other Halāl medicines are available. (Ma'āriful Qur'ān, Vol.1 pg. 426-427)

It is stated in Durrul Mukhtār that the Fuqahā have differed regarding seeking a cure through Harām products. The stronger verdict is that it is Harām. However, the present Ulamā have given permission if it is discovered that the Harām product is the only cure, and no other medicine is known.

Protein Drinks

Q Is it permissible to consume protein shakes?

A Protein powder is a supplementary dietary compound that is consumed in addition to food, in order to gain the adequate amount of nutrition and minerals for a person who regularly exercises and does weight lifting. This is so that when doing exercise, the body muscles obtain an increased amount of protein and minerals in addition to food, so that the muscles can grow efficiently. Protein powders generally contain whey, soy, rice and eggs. This is similar to consuming food, therefore, generally it would be permissible to consume as long as such protein powders/shakes do not contain any unlawful or impure ingredients. If so, then it would not be permissible for consumption and as a result, anything that is mixed with it, will also become impure and unlawful to consume.

Spirit Vinegar

Q Several food products such as mayonnaise, tomato sauce, mackerel fillets etc. contain spirit vinegar. What is spirit vinegar? Is it Halāl?

A Spirit vinegar is extracted from molasses (sugary substance). This is made into spirit by distillation and the substrate or residue is removed. It is called spirit because it is an alcoholic preparation with no characterizing components. It is then fermented completely into acetic acid. The product does not contain alcohol, as far as the research suggests. Since all of the characteristics of alcohol (i.e. intoxication) are removed, spirit vinegar thus becomes pure and permissible for consumption.

Q Is it permissible to have spirit vinegar? I have heard there is a difference of opinion on it. Some scholars say it is allowed due to the change but others say it is not because it is still alcohol?

A It is mentioned in the books of jurisprudence that if the compound structure of any substance changes to another substance then the ruling of that substance also changes. If alcohol was to change into vinegar to the extent that no traces of alcohol was to remain then the latter substance will be considered vinegar and permissible to use. So far as the latest research suggests that during the fermentation process, the characteristics of alcohol, such as intoxication are removed, hence making it lawful for consumption.

Note: The above ruling is based on the current research we did in answering the question. If future research suggests otherwise, then the ruling shall be revised. In this case, you must consult the scholars of its revised and new ruling.

Gelatine in Foods

Q Gelatine in food is labelled as either from pork or from bovine. Pork gelatine is Harām, but what about bovine?

A Bovine is derived from cattle, commonly from cows. If it is not slaughtered according to the Islamic method then it is necessary to abstain from consuming bovine gelatine.

Doubt in Food

Q If I have a doubt as to whether or not an item is Halāl or Harām and another Muslim brother says it is definitely Halāl but I am still not convinced as evidence is not shown to me, would it

be permissible for me to give this doubtful item to a brother who has no doubt about this item? Would I be sinful if I give it to him?

A Before I begin to answer this question, I would like to clarify the meaning of doubtful substances in the Shari'ah. Many people are unfortunately disturbed and agitated when it comes to doubtful sources because many Muslims are unaware of its Shar'ī implication and ruling.

Imām Tirmizi ※ has narrated a Hadīth in his Sunan, on the authority of Sayyidunā Nu'mān Ibn Bashīr ※, that the Holy Prophet ※ said, "Halāl is clear and Harām is clear and between them are (many) doubtful matters which many people are unaware of whether they are Halāl or Harām. So, whosoever was to forsake them (doubtful things) for the sake of his Dīn and honour then indeed he is safeguarded. However, whosoever indulges in them (doubtful matters), then it is highly possible that he may indulge in Harām."

Shaykh Mufti Taqi Uthmāni Sāhib comments on this Hadīth quite extensively in his commentary of Tirmizi. In summary, the ruling of abstaining from doubtful sources depends on different circumstances and evidences presented from both sides. Sometimes, to abstain from doubtful products is compulsory whilst sometimes it is Mustahab (desirable). There are two scenarios to this issue;

1. If there is a product with the possibility of being either Halāl or Harām, then the jurists and scholars will first analyze evidences of

both sides and give a ruling accordingly. But if it is difficult to reach a decisive conclusion due to the balance of evidences of both sides, then the matter will be classed as **ambiguous and doubtful**. In this regard the scholar will issue a Fatwa of it being impermissible because the product is now a doubtful source.

It is stated in Al-Ashbāh wan-Nadhā'ir: When (the evidence of) Halāl and Harām are equal, then Harām will be given preference.

2. If regarding a product, the evidences of Halāl and Harām are presented but the evidences of Halāl are more weightier and convincing to the Mufti, then he will issue a verdict of it being Halāl. However, since there are some evidences of it being Harām, it would be preferable to abstain from this although it is still permissible to consume.

The above was to merely clarify the meaning of doubtful substances in the Shari'ah. Now coming to your question, the general ruling in this matter would be that it is the sacred right of every Muslim that one entertains a good impression of him.

Allāh 🙵 says, **"O you who believe! Abstain from many (forms of) suspicion; verily some forms of suspicion is a sin."** [49:12)]

It is understood from this verse that we must always abstain from being suspicious about a certain thing unless substantial evidence is presented before us. Hence, if a Muslim brother was to inform you of a certain product to be permissible, provided that he is gen-

35

uine, honest, trustworthy and reliable, then we can take such a person's statement at face value. To have doubts thereafter would lead to suspicion. Remember, there is a big difference between the Islamic concept of Shubh (doubtful product) and suspicion.

Doubtful matter, as explained previously is when evidences from both sides are equal to the extent that it is difficult to give preference to one side. Thus, the Shar'ī ruling would be to abstain from the matter because it falls into the category of Shubuhāt (ambiguous matters), whereas, suspicion is from Shaytān and must be avoided.

To further endorse this, it is mentioned in a Hadīth which is related by Sayyidah Ā'ishah ﷺ that once a group of people came and informed the Holy Prophet ﷺ that some people presented meat but we do not know whether it was slaughtered with Allāh's ﷻ Name mentioned or not? The Holy Prophet ﷺ replied, "Consume it by reciting the Name of Allāh ﷻ upon it." Sayyidah Ā'ishah ﷺ states that those people (regarding whom the people enquired about) were very close to their time of Kufr (i.e. they recently embraced Islām). (Bukhāri)

According to Shaykh Mufti Taqi Uthmāni, this Hadīth does not stand as evidence for any meat to become Halāl when it is absolutely certain that the slaughterer deliberately omitted the name of Allāh ﷻ when slaughtering (because such animal will become Harām to consume). Rather, the most that is established from this Hadīth is that if any Muslim was to bring meat to consume then it is obvious that he would slaughter it according to the Shari'ah and the external impression would be considered. We have been commanded (through this Hadīth) to entertain good impression regarding a Muslim; if he was to present meat to us, then it is not necessary to investigate further. (Fiqhi-Maqālāt)

Although this is concerning meat, the basic core lesson inferred from this is that we must harbour a good impression regarding every Muslim unless proven otherwise. Therefore, if a genuine and reliable Muslim informs you of a particular thing to be Halāl, then still having doubts about that thing will not constitute as Shubuhāt (doubtful matters) and neither will it render that thing to be Harām.

Nevertheless, once something has been proven to be Harām or doubtful then it would not only be necessary to abstain from it but it would also not be permissible to give to someone else.

As an additional point, Shaykh Mufti Taqi Uthmāni Sāhib states an important principle about Halāl and Harām. He mentions that meat in origin is Harām and anything else in origin apart from meat is Halāl. Anything besides meat would be permissible to consume unless there is substantial proof of it being Harām. For instance, a chapatti is regarded as Halāl even if a non-Muslim gives it to us to eat unless there is substantial evidence to prove that impurity or Harām ingredients has been added to it. Mere speculation would not render it totally Harām.

On the contrary, meat in essence is Harām unless there is substantial evidence (which includes the information of a trustworthy, honest and reliable Muslim to inform) that it has been slaughtered according to the Shari'ah. (Taqrīr Tirmizi)

Other titles from JKN PUBLICATIONS

Your Questions Answered

An outstanding book written by Shaykh Mufti Saiful Islām. A very comprehensive yet simple Fatāwa book and a source of guidance that reaches out to a wider audience i.e. the English speaking Muslims. The reader will benefit from the various answers to questions based on the Laws of Islām relating to the beliefs of Islām, knowledge, Sunnah, pillars of Islām, marriage, divorce and contemporary issues.

UK RRP: £7.50

Hadīth for Beginners

A concise Hadīth book with various Ahādeeth that relate to basic Ibādāh and moral etiquettes in Islām accessible to a wider readership. Each Hadīth has been presented with the Arabic text, its translation and commentary to enlighten the reader, its meaning and application in day-to-day life.

UK RRP: £3.00

Du'ā for Beginners

This book contains basic Du'ās which every Muslim should recite on a daily basis. Highly recommended to young children and adults studying at Islamic schools and Madrasahs so that one may cherish the beautiful treasure of supplications of our beloved Prophet ﷺ in one's daily life, which will ultimately bring peace and happiness in both worlds, Inshā-Allāh.

UK RRP: £2.00

How well do you know Islām?

An exciting educational book which contains 300 multiple questions and answers to help you increase your knowledge on Islām! Ideal for the whole family, especially children and adult students to learn new knowledge in an enjoyable way and cherish the treasures of knowledge that you will acquire from this book. A very beneficial tool for educational syllabus.

UK RRP: £3.00

Treasures of the Holy Qur'ān

This book entitled "Treasures of the Holy Qur'ān" has been compiled to create a stronger bond between the Holy Qur'ān and the readers. It mentions the different virtues of Sūrahs and verses from the Holy Qur'ān with the hope that the readers will increase their zeal and enthusiasm to recite and inculcate the teachings of the Holy Qur'ān into their daily lives.

UK RRP: £3.00

Other titles from JKN PUBLICATIONS

Marriage - A Complete Solution
Islām regards marriage as a great act of worship. This book has been designed to provide the fundamental teachings and guidelines of all what relates to the marital life in a simplified English language. It encapsulates in a nutshell all the marriage laws mentioned in many of the main reference books in order to facilitate their understanding and implementation.

UK RRP: £5.00

Pearls of Luqmān
This book is a comprehensive commentary of Sūrah Luqmān, written beautifully by Shaykh Mufti Saiful Islām. It offers the reader with an enquiring mind, abundance of advice, guidance, counselling and wisdom.

The reader will be enlightened by many wonderful topics and anecdotes mentioned in this book, which will create a greater understanding of the Holy Qur'ān and its wisdom. The book highlights some of the wise sayings and words of advice Luqmān ﷺ gave to his son.

UK RRP: £3.00

Arabic Grammar Beginners
This book is a study of Arabic Grammar based on the subject of Nahw (Syntax) in a simplified English format. If a student studies this book thoroughly, he/she will develop a very good foundation in this field, Inshā-Allāh. Many books have been written on this subject in various languages such as Arabic, Persian and Urdu. However, in this day and age there is a growing demand for this subject to be available in English .

UK RRP: £3.00

A Gift to My Youngsters
This treasure filled book, is a collection of Islamic stories, morals and anecdotes from the life of our beloved Prophet ﷺ, his Companions ﷺ and the pious predecessors. The stories and anecdotes are based on moral and ethical values, which the reader will enjoy sharing with their peers, friends, families and loved ones.

"A Gift to My Youngsters" – is a wonderful gift presented to the readers personally, by the author himself, especially with the youngsters in mind. He has carefully selected stories and anecdotes containing beautiful morals, lessons and valuable knowledge and wisdom.

UK RRP: £5.00

Travel Companion

The beauty of this book is that it enables a person on any journey, small or distant or simply at home, to utilise their spare time to read and benefit from an exciting and vast collection of important and interesting Islamic topics and lessons. Written in simple and easy to read text, this book will immensely benefit both the newly interested person in Islām and the inquiring mind of a student expanding upon their existing knowledge. Inspiring reminders from the Holy Qur'ān and the blessed words of our beloved Prophet ﷺ beautifies each topic and will illuminate the heart of the reader. **UK RRP: £5.00**

Pearls of Wisdom

Junaid Baghdādī ﷺ once said, "Allāh ﷻ strengthens through these Islamic stories the hearts of His friends, as proven from the Qur'anic verse, **"And all that We narrate unto you of the stories of the Messengers, so as to strengthen through it your heart."** (11:120) Mālik Ibn Dinār ﷺ stated that such stories are gifts from Paradise. He also emphasised to narrate these stories as much as possible as they are gems and it is possible that an individual might find a truly rare and invaluable gem among them. **UK RRP: £6.00**

Inspirations

This book contains a compilation of selected speeches delivered by Shaykh Mufti Saiful Islām on a variety of topics such as the Holy Qur'ān, Nikāh and eating Halāl. Having previously been compiled in separate booklets, it was decided that the transcripts be gathered together in one book for the benefit of the reader. In addition to this, we have included in this book, further speeches which have not yet been printed.

UK RRP: £6.00

Gift to my Sisters

A thought provoking compilation of very interesting articles including real life stories of pious predecessors, imaginative illustrations and much more. All designed to influence and motivate mothers, sisters, wives and daughters towards an ideal Islamic lifestyle. A lifestyle referred to by our Creator, Allāh ﷻ in the Holy Qur'ān as the means to salvation and ultimate success. **UK RRP: £6.00**

Gift to my Brothers

A thought provoking compilation of very interesting articles including real life stories of pious predecessors, imaginative illustrations, medical advices on intoxicants and rehabilitation and much more. All designed to influence and motivate fathers, brothers, husbands and sons towards an ideal Islamic lifestyle. A lifestyle referred to by our Creator, Allāh ﷻ in the Holy Qur'ān as the means to salvation and ultimate success.

UK RRP: £5.00

Heroes of Islām

"In the narratives there is certainly a lesson for people of intelligence (understanding)." (12:111)

A fine blend of Islamic personalities who have been recognised for leaving a lasting mark in the hearts and minds of people.

A distinguishing feature of this book is that the author has selected not only some of the most world and historically famous renowned scholars but also these lesser known and a few who have simply left behind a valuable piece of advice to their nearest and dearest. **UK RRP: £5.00**

Ask a Mufti (3 volumes)

Muslims in every generation have confronted different kinds of challenges. Inspite of that, Islām produced such luminary Ulamā who confronted and responded to the challenges of their time to guide the Ummah to the straight path. "Ask A Mufti" is a comprehensive three volume fatwa book, based on the Hanafi School, covering a wide range of topics related to every aspect of human life such as belief, ritual worship, life after death and contemporary legal topics related to purity, commercial transaction, marriage, divorce, food, cosmetic, laws pertaining to women, Islamic medical ethics and much more.

UK RRP: £30.00

Should I Follow a Madhab?

Taqleed or following one of the four legal schools is not a new phenomenon. Historically, scholars of great calibre and luminaries, each one being a specialist in his own right, were known to have adhered to one of the four legal schools. It is only in the previous century that a minority group emerged advocating a severe ban on following one of the four major schools.

This book endeavours to address the topic of Taqleed and elucidates its importance and necessity in this day and age. It will also, by the Divine Will of Allāh ﷻ dispel some of the confusion surrounding this topic. **UK RRP: £5.00**

Advice for the Students of Knowledge

Allāh ﷻ describes divine knowledge in the Holy Qur'ān as a 'Light'. Amongst the qualities of light are purity and guidance. The Holy Prophet ﷺ has clearly explained this concept in many blessed Ahādeeth and has also taught us many supplications in which we ask for beneficial knowledge.

This book is a golden tool for every sincere student of knowledge wishing to mould his/her character and engrain those correct qualities in order to be worthy of receiving the great gift of Ilm from Allāh ﷻ. **UK RRP: £3.00**

Stories for Children

"Stories for Children" - is a wonderful gift presented to the readers personally by the author himself, especially with the young children in mind. The stories are based on moral and ethical values, which the reader will enjoy sharing with their peers, friends, families and loved ones. The aim is to present to the children stories and incidents which contain moral lessons, in order to reform and correct their lives, according to the Holy Qur'ān and Sunnah.

UK RRP: £5.00

Pearls from My Shaykh

This book contains a collection of pearls and inspirational accounts of the Holy Prophet ﷺ, his noble Companions, pious predecessors and some personal accounts and sayings of our well-known contemporary scholar and spiritual guide, Shaykh Mufti Saiful Islām Sāhib. Each anecdote and narrative of the pious predecessors have been written in the way that was narrated by Mufti Saiful Islām Sāhib in his discourses, drawing the specific lessons he intended from telling the story. The accounts from the life of the Shaykh has been compiled by a particular student based on their own experience and personal observation. **UK RRP: £5.00**

Paradise & Hell

This book is a collection of detailed explanation of Paradise and Hell including the state and conditions of its inhabitants. All the details have been taken from various reliable sources. The purpose of its compilation is for the reader to contemplate and appreciate the innumerable favours, rewards, comfort and unlimited luxuries of Paradise and at the same time take heed from the punishment of Hell. Shaykh Mufti Saiful Islām Sāhib has presented this book in a unique format by including the Tafseer and virtues of Sūrah Ar-Rahmān. **UK RRP: £5.00**

Prayers for Forgiveness

Prayers for Forgiveness' is a short compilation of Du'ās in Arabic with English translation and transliteration. This book can be studied after 'Du'ā for Beginners' or as a separate book. It includes twenty more Du'ās which have not been mentioned in the previous Du'ā book. It also includes a section of Du'ās from the Holy Qur'ān and a section from the Ahādeeth. The book concludes with a section mentioning the Ninety-Nine Names of Allāh ﷻ with its translation and transliteration. **UK RRP: £3.00**

Scattered Pearls

This book is a collection of scattered pearls taken from books, magazines, emails and WhatsApp messages. These pearls will hopefully increase our knowledge, wisdom and make us realise the purpose of life. In this book, Mufti Sāhib has included messages sent to him from scholars, friends and colleagues which will be beneficial and interesting for our readers Inshā-Allāh. **UK RRP: £4.00**

Poems of Wisdom

This book is a collection of poems from those who contributed to the Al-Mumin Magazine in the poems section. The Hadeeth mentions "Indeed some form of poems are full of wisdom." The themes of each poem vary between wittiness, thought provocation, moral lessons, emotional to name but a few. The readers will benefit from this immensely and make them ponder over the outlook of life in general.

UK RRP: £4.00

Horrors of Judgement Day

This book is a detailed and informative commentary of the first three Sūrahs of the last Juz namely; Sūrah Naba, Sūrah Nāzi'āt and Sūrah Abasa. These Sūrahs vividly depict the horrific events and scenes of the Great Day in order to warn mankind the end of this world. These Sūrahs are an essential reminder for us all to instil the fear and concern of the Day of Judgement and to detach ourselves from the worldly pleasures. Reading this book allows us to attain the true realization of this world and provides essential advices of how to gain eternal salvation in the Hereafter.

RRP: £5:00

Spiritual Heart

It is necessary that Muslims always strive to better themselves at all times and to free themselves from the destructive maladies. This book focusses on three main spiritual maladies; pride, anger and evil gazes. It explains its root causes and offers some spiritual cures. Many examples from the lives of the pious predecessors are used for inspiration and encouragement for controlling the above three maladies. It is hoped that the purification process of the heart becomes easy once the underlying roots of the above maladies are clearly understood.   **UK RRP: £5:00**

Hajj & Umrah for Beginners

This book is a step by step guide on Hajj and Umrah for absolute beginners. Many other additional important rulings (Masāil) have been included that will Insha-Allāh prove very useful for our readers. The book also includes some etiquettes of visiting (Ziyārat) of the Holy Prophet's ﷺ blessed Masjid and his Holy Grave.

UK RRP £3:00

Advice for the Spiritual Travellers

This book contains essential guidelines for a spiritual Murīd to gain some familiarity of the science of Tasawwuf. It explains the meaning and aims of Tasawwuf, some understanding around the concept of the soul, and general guidelines for a spiritual Murīd. This is highly recommended book and it is hoped that it gains wider readership among those Murīds who are basically new to the science of Tasawwuf.

UK RRP £3:00

Don't Worry Be Happy

This book is a compilation of sayings and earnest pieces of advice that have been gathered directly from my respected teacher Shaykh Mufti Saiful Islām Sāhib. The book consists of many valuable enlightenments including how to deal with challenges of life, promoting unity, practicing good manners, being optimistic and many other valuable advices. Our respected Shaykh has gathered this Naseehah from meditating, contemplating, analysing and searching for the gems within Qur'anic verses, Ahādeeth and teachings of our Pious Predecessors. **UK RRP £1:00**

Kanzul Bāri

Kanzul Bāri provides a detailed commentary of the Ahādeeth contained in Saheeh al-Bukhāri. The commentary includes Imām Bukhāri's ﷺ biography, the status of his book, spiritual advice, inspirational accounts along with academic discussions related to Fiqh, its application and differences of opinion. Moreover, it answers objections arising in one's mind about certain Ahādeeth. Inquisitive students of Hadeeth will find this commentary a very useful reference book in the final year of their Ālim course for gaining a deeper understanding of the science of Hadeeth. **UK RRP: £15.00**

How to Become a Friend of Allāh ﷺ

The friends of Allāh ﷺ have been described in detail in the Holy Qur'ān and Āhadeeth. This book endeavours its readers to help create a bond with Allāh ﷺ in attaining His friendship as He is the sole Creator of all material and immaterial things. It is only through Allāh's ﷺ friendship, an individual will achieve happiness in this life and the Hereafter, hence eliminate worries, sadness, depression, anxiety and misery of this world. **UK RRP:**

Gems & Jewels

This book contains a selection of articles which have been gathered for the benefit of the readers covering a variety of topics on various aspects of daily life. It offers precious advice and anecdotes that contain moral lessons. The advice captivates its readers and will extend the narrowness of their thoughts to deep reflection, wisdom and appreciation of the purpose of our existence. **UK RRP: £4.00**

End of Time

This book is a comprehensive explanation of the three Sūrahs of Juzz Amma; Sūrah Takweer, Sūrah Infitār and Sūrah Mutaffifeen. This book is a continuation from the previous book of the same author, 'Horrors of Judgement Day'. The three Sūrahs vividly sketch out the scene of the Day of Judgement and describe the state of both the inmates of Jannah and Jahannam. Mufti Saiful Islām Sāhib provides an easy but comprehensive commentary of the three Sūrahs facilitating its understanding for the readers whilst capturing the horrific scene of the ending of the world and the conditions of mankind on that horrific Day. **UK RRP: £5.00**

Andalus (modern day Spain), the long lost history, was once a country that produced many great calibre of Muslim scholars comprising of Mufassirūn, Muhaddithūn, Fuqahā, judges, scientists, philosophers, surgeons, to name but a few. The Muslims conquered Andalus in 711 AD and ruled over it for eight-hundred years. This was known as the era of Muslim glory. Many non-Muslim Europeans during that time travelled to Spain to study under Muslim scholars. The remanences of the Muslim rule in Spain are manifested through their universities, magnificent palaces and Masājid carved with Arabic writings, standing even until today. In this book, Shaykh Mufti Saiful Islām shares some of his valuable experiences he witnessed during his journey to Spain. **UK RRP: £3.00**

Ideal Youth

This book contains articles gathered from various social media avenues; maga-zines, emails, WhatsApp and telegram messages that provide useful tips of ad-vice for those who have the zeal to learn and consider changing their negative habits and behavior and become better Muslims to set a positive trend for the next generation. **UK RRP:£4:00**

Ideal Teacher

This book contains abundance of precious advices for the Ulamā who are in the teaching profession. It serves to present Islamic ethical principles of teaching and to remind every teacher of their moral duties towards their students. This book will Inshā-Allāh prove to be beneficial for newly graduates and scholars wanting to utilize their knowledge through teaching. **UK RRP:£4:00**

Ideal Student

This book is a guide for all students of knowledge in achieving the excellent qualities of becoming an ideal student. It contains precious advices, anecdotes of our pious predecessors and tips in developing good morals as a student. Good morals is vital for seeking knowledge. A must for all students if they want to develop their Islamic Knowledge. **UK RRP:£4:00**

Ideal Parents

This book contains a wealth of knowledge in achieving the qualities of becoming ideal parents. It contains precious advices, anecdotes of our pious predecessors and tips in developing good parenthood skills. Good morals is vital for seeking knowledge. A must for all parents . **UK RRP:£4:00**

Ideal Couple

This book is a compilation of inspiring stories and articles containing useful tips and life skills for every couple. Marriage life is a big responsibility and success in marriage is only possible if the couple know what it means to be an ideal couple. **UK RRP:£4:00**

Ideal Role Model

This book is a compilation of sayings and accounts of our pious prede-cessors. The purpose of this book is so we can learn from our pious predecessors the purpose of this life and how to attain closer to the Creator. Those people who inspires us attaining closeness to our Crea-tor are our true role models. A must everyone to read. **UK RRP:£4:00**

Bangladesh– A Land of Natural Beauty

This book is a compilation of our respected Shaykh's journeys to Bangladesh including visits to famous Madāris and Masājid around the country. The Shaykh shares some of his thought provoking experiences and his personal visits with great scholars in Bangla-desh. **UK RRP: £4.00**

...arls from the Qur'an

...is series begins with the small Sūrahs from 30th Juzz initially, ...ravelling its heavenly gems, precious advices and anecdotes ...rthy of personal reflection. It will most definitely benefit both ...ose new to as well as advanced students of the science of Tafsīr. ...e purpose is to make it easily accessible for the general public in ...derstanding the meaning of the Holy Qur'ān. **UK RRP: £10.00**

When the Heavens Split

This book contains the commentary of four Sūrahs from Juzz Amma name-ly; Sūrah Inshiqāq, Sūrah Burūj, Sūrah Tāriq and Sūrah A'lā. The first two Sūrahs contain a common theme of capturing the scenes and events of the Last Day and how this world will come to an end. However, all four Sūrahs mentioned, have a connection of the journey of humanity, reflection on nature, how nature changes and most importantly, giving severe warnings to mankind about the punishments and exhorting them to prepare for the Hereafter through good deeds and refraining from sins. **UK RRP: £4.00**